The Poetry of Dante Gabriel Rossetti

VOLUME II

Dante Gabriel Rossetti was born on May 12th 1828 in London, England.

The young Gabriel Charles Dante Rossetti was the son of émigré Italian scholar Gabriele Pasquale Giuseppe Rossetti and his wife Frances Polidori.

To family and friends he was Gabriel, but in print he put the name Dante first (in honour of Dante Alighieri). It was an artistic family of siblings; he was the brother of famed poet Christina Rossetti, critic William Michael Rossetti, and author Maria Francesca Rossetti. During his early years Rossetti was home educated and spent hours immersed reading the Bible, Shakespeare, Dickens, Scott and Byron.

As a youth he was described as "self-possessed, articulate, passionate and charismatic" but also "ardent, poetic and feckless". He attended King's College School. Like his siblings he most wished to be a poet but had a keen eye as a painter, having shown a great interest in Medieval Italian art.

His education continued at Henry Sass's Drawing Academy from 1841 to 1845 and he then enrolled at the Antique School of the Royal Academy, until 1848. After leaving the Royal Academy, Rossetti studied under Ford Madox Brown, with whom he remained close throughout his life.

Following the exhibition of William Holman Hunt's painting The Eve of St. Agnes, Rossetti sought out Hunt's friendship. The painting based on the poem by Keats and Rossetti's own poem, "The Blessed Damozel", was an imitation of Keats, and he believed Hunt might therefore share his artistic and literary ideals.

He did. Together they developed and founded the philosophy of the Pre-Raphaelite Brotherhood together with John Everett Millais.

They had high ideals; to reform English art by rejecting the mechanistic approach first adopted by the Mannerists who succeeded Raphael and Michelangelo and the formal training introduced by Sir Joshua Reynolds. Their hope was to return to the detail, intense colours, and complex compositions of Quattrocento Italian and Flemish art.

The eminent critic John Ruskin wrote: "Every Pre-Raphaelite landscape background is painted to the last touch, in the open air, from the thing itself. Every Pre-Raphaelite figure, however studied in expression, is a true portrait of some living person".

The brotherhood's magazine, The Germ, was first published in 1850. Rossetti contributed a poem, "The Blessed Damozel", and a story about a fictional early Italian artist inspired by a vision of a woman who bids him combine the human and the divine in his art. Rossetti was always drawn to the medieval side of the movement, eagerly translating Dante and other medieval Italian poets, as well as adopting the stylistic characteristics of the early Italians.

Rossetti first met his future wife, Elizabeth Siddal in 1849, when she was modelling for Deverell. By 1851, she was sitting for Rossetti and they were involved in an intense relationship.

Rossetti's most abundant and personal works were pencil sketches of Lizzie at home that began in 1852 when he moved into Chatham Place with her. They became increasingly withdrawn, totally absorbed in each other. The lovers nicknamed each other; "Guggums" and "Dove". Rossetti also taught Lizzie to paint and write. She undoubtedly had talent.

Both Rossetti and others supported her work and amongst a small circle it was admired.

Lizzie however suffered from various health problems and Rossetti's treatment of her through liaisons with other women, despite an intense love for her, exacerbated her moods.

Despite plans and several attempts to marry, it was only on May 23rd 1860 at St Clement's Church in Hastings that the ceremony took place. There were no family or friends present, just witnesses whom they had found in Hastings.

Lizzie was so frail and ill that she had to be carried to the church. After the wedding, as soon as Lizzie was well enough, they left to honeymoon in France.

In 1861, Rossetti together with William Morris became a founding partner in the decorative arts firm, Morris, Marshall, Faulkner & Co. Rossetti contributed designs for stained glass and other decorative objects.

Meanwhile his marriage to Lizzie was troubled. The terrible hurt of Rossetti's affairs with other women had caused stress leading to depression and several other illnesses. She now began to take laudanum to which she became addicted.

During 1861, Lizzie became pregnant. She was overjoyed but the resulting birth was a stillborn daughter. The death left Lizzie with a post-partum depression.

Lizzie overdosed on laudanum in the early months of 1862. Rossetti discovered her unconscious and dying in bed some hours after they had had dinner with their friend Algernon Charles Swinburne.

Rossetti was devastated by her death, and, at her funeral, he buried the bulk of his unpublished poems with her at Highgate Cemetery.

Poetry and painting are closely entwined in Rossetti's work. His time was divided almost equally between them. He frequently wrote sonnets to accompany his pictures, spanning from The Girlhood of Mary Virgin (1849) and Astarte Syriaca (1877), while also creating art to illustrate poems such as "Goblin Market" by his sister.

Rossetti's personal life was closely woven into his work, especially his relationships with his models and muses; Lizzie, Fanny Cornforth and the wife of William Morris, Jane.

Jane Morris, regularly sat for him during the next few years, and it was said she "consumed and obsessed him in paint, poetry, and life".

In 1869, William Morris and Rossetti rented a country house, Kelmscott Manor at Kelmscott, Oxfordshire, as a summer home, but it also became a retreat for Rossetti and Jane Morris to have a long-lasting and complicated liaison.

During these years, Rossetti was prevailed upon by friends to exhume his poems from his wife's grave which he eventually did, collating and publishing them in 1870 in the volume Poems by D. G. Rossetti.

The controversy on their publication was intense. Their eroticism and sensuality caused offence. One poem, "Nuptial Sleep", described a couple falling asleep after sex. It was part of Rossetti's sonnet sequence The House of Life, a complex series of poems tracing the physical and spiritual development of an intimate relationship.

Rossetti beautifully described the sonnet form as a "moment's monument". The House of Life was a series of interacting monuments to these moments – an elaborate whole made from a mosaic of intensely described fragments. It was Rossetti's crowning literary achievement.

The critical savaging together with the complications of his relationship with Jane Morris contributed to a mental breakdown in June 1872, and although he joined Jane at Kelmscott that September, he "spent his days in a haze of chloral and whisky".

The next summer he was much improved, and both Alexa Wilding and Jane sat for him at Kelmscott, where he created a soulful series of dream-like portraits.

In 1874, William Morris re-organised his decorative arts firm, cutting Rossetti out of the business. Rossetti, again staying at Kelmscott, when he heard the news, abruptly left in July 1874 never to return.

Toward the end of his life, he sank into a morbid state, shadowed by addiction to chloral hydrate and increasing mental instability. He spent his last years as a recluse at Cheyne Walk.

In 1881, Rossetti published a second volume of poems, Ballads and Sonnets, which included the remaining sonnets from The House of Life sequence.

On Easter Sunday, April 9th, 1882, he died at the country house of a friend, where he had gone in a vain attempt to recover his health, which had been destroyed by chloral.

The actual cause of death was by Bright's Disease, a kidney disease. Rossetti had been housebound for some years with paralysis of the legs, though his chloral addiction is believed to have been a means of alleviating pain from a botched hydrocele (the accumulation of fluid in a body cavity or sac) removal. He had been suffering from alcohol psychosis for some time brought on by the excessive whisky consumption used to drown out the very bitter taste of the chloral hydrate.

He is buried at Birchington-on-Sea, Kent, England.

Index of Contents
The Blessed Damozel
Love's Nocturn

Last Sonnets at Paris
Beauty and the Bird
Percy Bysshe Shelley
Thomas Chatterton
On Burns
Blake
On Christina Rossetti
Shakespeare
John Keats
An Epitaph for Keats
Samuel Taylor Coleridge
On William Morris
St Wagner's Eve
Dante at Verona
The Ballad of Dead Ladies
Three Shadows
The Orchard-Pit
The English Revolution of 1848
Wellington's Funeral
In The Train, And at Versailles
On the Road to Waterloo: 17 October (En Vigilante, 2 Hours)
Antwerp and Bruges
At the Station of the Versailles Railway
Between Ghent and Bruges
L'envoi: Brussels, Hotel Du Midi
At the Sunrise, 1848
Sunset Wings
English May
A Little While
The Sin of Detection
A Bitter Song to His Lady
Ladies That Have Intelligence in Love
First Love Remembered
Genius in Beauty
Our Lady of the Rocks by Leonardo da Vinci
The Portrait
Joan of Arc
Vox Ecclesiae, Vox Christi
After the French Liberation of Italy
After the German Subjugation of France, 1871
The White Ship Henry I of England—25th November 1120
On Refusal of Aid Between Nations
Words on the Window Pane
Parted Presence
Sacrament Hymn
Chimes
Venus Verticordia (For A Picture)
Penumbra

Hidden Harmony
Insomnia
Aspecta Medusa (for a Drawing)
Jenny

The Blessed Damozel

The blessed damozel leaned out
From the gold bar of Heaven;
Her eyes were deeper than the depth
Of waters stilled at even;
She had three lilies in her hand,
And the stars in her hair were seven.

Her robe, ungirt from clasp to hem,
No wrought flowers did adorn,
But a white rose of Mary's gift,
For service meetly worn;
Her hair that lay along her back
Was yellow like ripe corn.

Herseemed she scarce had been a day
One of God's choristers;
The wonder was not yet quite gone
From that still look of hers;
Albeit, to them she left, her day
Had counted as ten years.

(To one, it is ten years of years.
. . . Yet now, and in this place,
Surely she leaned o'er me—her hair
Fell all about my face. . . .
Nothing: the autumn fall of leaves.
The whole year sets apace.)

It was the rampart of God's house
That she was standing on;
By God built over the sheer depth
The which is Space begun;
So high, that looking downward thence
She scarce could see the sun.

It lies in Heaven, across the flood
Of ether, as a bridge.
Beneath, the tides of day and night

With flame and darkness ridge
The void, as low as where this earth
Spins like a fretful midge.

Around her, lovers, newly met
In joy no sorrow claims,
Spoke evermore among themselves
Their rapturous new names;
And the souls mounting up to God
Went by her like thin flames.

And still she bowed herself and stooped
Out of the circling charm;
Until her bosom must have made
The bar she leaned on warm,
And the lilies lay as if asleep
Along her bended arm.

From the fixed place of Heaven she saw
Time like a pulse shake fierce
Through all the worlds. Her gaze still strove
Within the gulf to pierce
Its path; and now she spoke as when
The stars sang in their spheres.

The sun was gone now; the curled moon
Was like a little feather
Fluttering far down the gulf; and now
She spoke through the still weather.
Her voice was like the voice the stars
Had when they sang together.

(Ah sweet! Even now, in that bird's song,
Strove not her accents there,
Fain to be hearkened? When those bells
Possessed the mid-day air,
Strove not her steps to reach my side
Down all the echoing stair?)

'I wish that he were come to me,
For he will come,' she said.
'Have I not prayed in Heaven?—on earth,
Lord, Lord, has he not pray'd?
Are not two prayers a perfect strength?
And shall I feel afraid?

'When round his head the aureole clings,
And he is clothed in white,

I'll take his hand and go with him
To the deep wells of light;
We will step down as to a stream,
And bathe there in God's sight.

'We two will stand beside that shrine,
Occult, withheld, untrod,
Whose lamps are stirred continually
With prayer sent up to God;
And see our old prayers, granted, melt
Each like a little cloud.

'We two will lie i'the shadow of
That living mystic tree
Within whose secret growth the Dove
Is sometimes felt to be,
While every leaf that His plumes touch
Saith His Name audibly.

'And I myself will teach to him,
I myself, lying so,
The songs I sing here; which his voice
Shall pause in, hushed and slow,
And find some knowledge at each pause,
Or some new thing to know.'

(Alas! We two, we two, thou say'st!
Yea, one wast thou with me
That once of old. But shall God lift
To endless unity
The soul whose likeness with thy soul
Was but its love for thee?)

'We two,' she said, 'will seek the groves
Where the lady Mary is,
With her five handmaidens, whose names
Are five sweet symphonies,
Cecily, Gertrude, Magdalen,
Margaret and Rosalys.

'Circlewise sit they, with bound locks
And foreheads garlanded;
Into the fine cloth white like flame
Weaving the golden thread,
To fashion the birth-robes for them
Who are just born, being dead.

'He shall fear, haply, and be dumb:

Then will I lay my cheek
To his, and tell about our love,
Not once abashed or weak:
And the dear Mother will approve
My pride, and let me speak.

'Herself shall bring us, hand in hand,
To Him round whom all souls
Kneel, the clear-ranged unnumbered heads
Bowed with their aureoles:
And angels meeting us shall sing
To their citherns and citoles.

'There will I ask of Christ the Lord
Thus much for him and me:—
Only to live as once on earth
With Love,—only to be,
As then awhile, for ever now
Together, I and he.'

She gazed and listened and then said,
Less sad of speech than mild,—
'All this is when he comes.' She ceased.
The light thrilled towards her, fill'd
With angels in strong level flight.
Her eyes prayed, and she smil'd.

(I saw her smile.) But soon their path
Was vague in distant spheres:
And then she cast her arms along
The golden barriers,
And laid her face between her hands,
And wept. (I heard her tears.)

Love's Nocturn

Master of the murmuring courts
Where the shapes of sleep convene!—
Lo! my spirit here exhorts
All the powers of thy demesne
For their aid to woo my queen.
What reports
Yield thy jealous courts unseen?

Vaporous, unaccountable,
Dreamland lies forlorn of light,

Hollow like a breathing shell.
Ah! that from all dreams I might
Choose one dream and guide its flight!
I know well
What her sleep should tell to-night.

There the dreams are multitudes:
Some whose buoyance waits not sleep,
Deep within the August woods;
Some that hum while rest may steep
Weary labour laid a-heap;
Interludes,
Some, of grievous moods that weep.

Poets' fancies all are there:
There the elf-girls flood with wings
Valleys full of plaintive air;
There breathe perfumes; there in rings
Whirl the foam-bewildered springs;
Siren there
Winds her dizzy hair and sings.

Thence the one dream mutually
Dreamed in bridal unison,
Less than waking ecstasy;
Half-formed visions that make moan
In the house of birth alone;
And what we
At death's wicket see, unknown.

But for mine own sleep, it lies
In one gracious form's control,
Fair with honorable eyes,
Lamps of an auspicious soul:
O their glance is loftiest dole,
Sweet and wise,
Wherein Love descries his goal.

Reft of her, my dreams are all
Clammy trance that fears the sky:
Changing footpaths shift and fall;
From polluted coverts nigh,
Miserable phantoms sigh;
Quakes the pall,
And the funeral goes by.

Master, is it soothly said
That, as echoes of man's speech

Far in secret clefts are made,
So do all men's bodies reach
Shadows o'er thy sunken beach,—
Shape or shade
In those halls pourtrayed of each?

Ah! might I, by thy good grace
Groping in the windy stair,
(Darkness and the breath of space
Like loud waters everywhere,)
Meeting mine own image there
Face to face,
Send it from that place to her!

Nay, not I; but oh! do thou,
Master, from thy shadowkind
Call my body's phantom now:
Bid it bear its face declin'd
Till its flight her slumbers find,
And her brow
Feel its presence bow like wind.

Where in groves the gracile Spring
Trembles, with mute orison
Confidently strengthening,
Water's voice and wind's as one
Shed an echo in the sun.
Soft as Spring,
Master, bid it sing and moan.

Song shall tell how glad and strong
Is the night she soothes alway;
Moan shall grieve with that parched tongue
Of the brazen hours of day:
Sounds as of the springtide they,
Moan and song,
While the chill months long for May.

Not the prayers which with all leave
The world's fluent woes prefer,—
Not the praise the world doth give,
Dulcet fulsome whisperer;—
Let it yield my love to her,
And achieve
Strength that shall not grieve or err.

Wheresoe'er my dreams befall,
Both at night-watch, (let it say,)

And where round the sundial
The reluctant hours of day,
Heartless, hopeless of their way,
Rest and call;—
There her glance doth fall and stay.

Suddenly her face is there:
So do mounting vapours wreathe
Subtle-scented transports where
The black firwood sets its teeth.
Part the boughs and look beneath,—
Lilies share
Secret waters there, and breathe.

Master, bid my shadow bend
Whispering thus till birth of light,
Lest new shapes that sleep may send
Scatter all its work to flight;—
Master, master of the night,
Bid it spend
Speech, song, prayer, and end aright.

Yet, ah me! if at her head
There another phantom lean
Murmuring o'er the fragrant bed,—
Ah! and if my spirit's queen
Smile those alien words between,—
Ah! poor shade!
Shall it strive, or fade unseen?

How should love's own messenger
Strive with love and be love's foe?
Master, nay! If thus, in her,
Sleep a wedded heart should show,—
Silent let mine image go,
Its old share
Of thy spell-bound air to know.

Like a vapour wan and mute,
Like a flame, so let it pass;
One low sigh across her lute,
One dull breath against her glass
And to my sad soul, alas!
One salute
Cold as when death's foot shall pass.

Then, too, let all hopes of mine,
All vain hopes by night and day,

Slowly at thy summoning sign
Rise up pallid and obey.
Dreams, if this is thus, were they:—
Be they thine,
And to dreamland pine away.

Yet from old time, life, not death,
Master, in thy rule is rife:
Lo! through thee, with mingling breath,
Adam woke beside his wife.
O Love bring me so, for strife,
Force and faith,
Bring me so not death but life!

Yea, to Love himself is pour'd
This frail song of hope and fear.
Thou art Love, of one accord
With kind Sleep to bring her near,
Still-eyed, deep-eyed, ah how dear!
Master, Lord,
In her name implor'd, O hear!

Last Sonnets at Paris

I

Chins that might serve the new Jerusalem;
Streets footsore; minute whisking milliners,
Dubbed graceful, but at whom one's eye demurs,
Knowing of England; ladies, much the same;
Bland smiling dogs with manes—a few of them
At pains to look like sporting characters;
Vast humming tabbies smothered in their furs;
Groseille, orgeat, meringues à la crême—
Good things to study; ditto bad—the maps
Of sloshy colour in the Louvre; cinq-francs
The largest coin; and at the restaurants
Large Ibrahim Pachas in Turkish caps
To pocket them. Un million d'habitants:
Cast up, they'll make an Englishman—perhaps.

II

Tiled floors in bedrooms; trees (now run to seed—
Such seed as the wind takes) of Liberty;
Squares with new names that no one seems to see;
Scrambling Briarean passages, which lead

To the first place you came from; urgent need
Of unperturbed nasal philosophy;
Through Paris (what with church and gallery)
Some forty first-rate paintings,—or indeed
Fifty mayhap; fine churches; splendid inns;
Fierce sentinels (toy-size without the stands)
Who spit their oaths at you and grind their r's
If at a fountain you would wash your hands;
One Frenchman (this is fact) who thinks he spars:—
Can even good dinners cover all these sins?

III
Yet in the mighty French metropolis
Our time has not gone from us utterly
In waste. The wise man saith, "An ample fee
For toil, to work thine end." Aye that it is.
Should England ask, "Was narrow prejudice
Stretched to its utmost point unflinchingly,
Even unto lying, at all times, by ye?"
We can say firmly: "Lord, thou knowest this,
Our soil may own us." Having but small French,
Hunt passed for a stern Spartan all the while,
Uncompromising, of few words: for me—
I think I was accounted generally
A fool, and just a little cracked. Thy smile
May light on us, Britannia, healthy wench.

Beauty and the Bird

She fluted with her mouth as when one sips,
And gently waved her golden head, inclin'd
Outside his cage close to the window-blind;
Till her fond bird, with little turns and dips,
Piped low to her of sweet companionships.
And when he made an end, some seed took she
And fed him from her tongue, which rosily
Peeped as a piercing bud between her lips.
And like the child in Chaucer, on whose tongue
The Blessed Mary laid, when he was dead,
A grain,—who straightway praised her name in song:
Even so, when she, a little lightly red,
Now turned on me and laughed, I heard the throng
Of inner voices praise her golden head.

Percy Bysshe Shelley

'Twixt those twin worlds,—the world of Sleep, which gave
No dream to warn,—the tidal world of Death,
Which the earth's sea, as the earth, replenisheth,—
Shelley, Song's orient sun, to breast the wave,
Rose from this couch that morn. Ah! did he brave
Only the sea?—or did man's deed of hell
Engulph his bark 'mid mists impenetrable? . . .
No eye discerned, nor any power might save.
When that mist cleared, O Shelley! what dread veil
Was rent for thee, to whom far-darkling Truth
Reigned sovereign guide through thy brief ageless youth?
Was the Truth thy Truth, Shelley?—Hush! All-Hail!
Past doubt, thou gav'st it; and in Truth's bright sphere
Art first of praisers, being most praisèd here.

Thomas Chatterton

With Shakspeare's manhood at a boy's wild heart,—
Through Hamlet's doubt to Shakspeare near allied,
And kin to Milton through his Satan's pride,—
At Death's sole door he stooped, and craved a dart;
And to the dear new bower of England's art,—
Even to that shrine Time else had deified,
The unuttered heart that soared against his side,—
Drove the fell point, and smote life's seals apart.
Thy nested home-loves, noble Chatterton;
The angel-trodden stair thy soul could trace
Up Redcliffe's spire; and in the world's armed space
Thy gallant sword-play:—these to many an one
Are sweet for ever; as thy grave unknown
And love-dream of thine unrecorded face.

On Burns

In whomsoe'er, since Poesy began,
A Poet most of all men we may scan,
Burns of all poets is the most a Man.

Blake

Epitaph

All beauty to pourtray,
Therein his duty lay,
And still through toilsome strife
Duty to him was life—
Most thankful still that duty
Lay in the paths of beauty.

On Christina Rossetti

There's a female bard, grim as a fakier,
Who daily grows shakier and shakier.

Shakespeare

Dear friend, if there be any bond
Which friendship wins not much beyond—
So old and fond, since thought began—
It may be that whose subtle span
Binds Shakespear to an English man.

John Keats

The weltering London ways where children weep
And girls whom none call maidens laugh,—strange road
Miring his outward steps, who inly trode
The bright Castalian brink and Latmos' steep:—
Even such his life's cross-paths; till deathly deep
He toiled through sands of Lethe; and long pain,
Weary with labour spurned and love found vain,
In dead Rome's sheltering shadow wrapped his sleep.
O pang-dowered Poet, whose reverberant lips
And heart-strung lyre awoke the Moon's eclipse,—
Thou whom the daisies glory in growing o'er,—
Their fragrance clings around thy name, not writ
But rumour'd in water, while the fame of it
Along Time's flood goes echoing evermore.

An Epitaph for Keats

Through one, years since hanged and forgot
Who stabbed backs by the Quarter,
Here lieth one who—while Time's stream
Runneth, as God hath taught her,
Bearing man's fame to men,—will have
His great name writ in water.

Samuel Taylor Coleridge

His Soul fared forth (as from the deep home-grove
The father-songster plies the hour-long quest),
To feed his soul-brood hungering in the nest;
But his warm Heart, the mother-bird, above
Their callow fledgling progeny still hove
With tented roof of wings and fostering breast
Till the Soul fed the soul-brood. Richly blest
From Heaven their growth, whose food was Human Love.
Yet ah! Like desert pools that show the stars
Once in long leagues,—even such the scarce-snatched hours
Which deepening pain left to his lordliest powers:—
Heaven lost through spider-trammelled prison-bars.
Six years, from sixty saved! Yet kindling skies
Own them, a beacon to our centuries.

On William Morris

Enter Skald, moored in a punt,
And jacks and tenches exeunt.

St Wagner's Eve

The hop—shop is shut up: the night doth wear.
Here, early, Collinson this evening fell
"Into the gulfs of sleep"; and Deverell
Has turned upon the pivot of his chair
The whole of this night long; and Hancock there
Has laboured to repeat, in accents screechy,
"Guardami ben, ben son, ben son Beatrice";
And Bernhard Smith still beamed, serene and square.
By eight, the coffee was all drunk. At nine
We gave the cat some milk. Our talk did shelve,

Ere ten, to gasps and stupor. Helpless grief
Made, towards eleven, my inmost spirit pine,
Knowing North's hour. And Hancock, hard on twelve,
Showed an engraving of his bas—relief.

Dante at Verona

Behold, even I, even I am Beatrice.
(Divine Comedy, Purgatory XXX)

Of Florence and of Beatrice
Servant and singer from of old,
O'er Dante's heart in youth had toll'd
The knell that gave his Lady peace;
And now in manhood flew the dart
Wherewith his City pierced his heart.
Yet if his Lady's home above
Was Heaven, on earth she filled his soul;
And if his City held control
To cast the body forth to rove,
The soul could soar from earth's vain throng,
And Heaven and Hell fulfil the song.
Follow his feet's appointed way;—
But little light we find that clears
The darkness of the exiled years.
Follow his spirit's journey:—nay,
What fires are blent, what winds are blown
On paths his feet may tread alone?
Yet of the twofold life he led
In chainless thought and fettered will
Some glimpses reach us,—somewhat still
Of the steep stairs and bitter bread,—
Of the soul's quest whose stern avow
For years had made him haggard now.
Alas! the Sacred Song whereto
Both heaven and earth had set their hand
Not only at Fame's gate did stand
Knocking to claim the passage through,
But toiled to ope that heavier door
Which Florence shut for evermore.
Shall not his birth's baptismal Town
One last high presage yet fulfil,
And at that font in Florence still
His forehead take the laurel-crown?
O God! or shall dead souls deny
The undying soul its prophecy?

Aye, 'tis their hour. Not yet forgot
The bitter words he spoke that day
When for some great charge far away
Her rulers his acceptance sought.
"And if I go, who stays?"—so rose
His scorn:—"and if I stay, who goes?"
"Lo! thou art gone now, and we stay"
(The curled lips mutter): "and no star
Is from thy mortal path so far
As streets where childhood knew the way.
To Heaven and Hell thy feet may win,
But thine own house they come not in."
Therefore, the loftier rose the song
To touch the secret things of God,
The deeper pierced the hate that trod
On base men's track who wrought the wrong;
Till the soul's effluence came to be
Its own exceeding agony.
Arriving only to depart,
From court to court, from land to land,
Like flame within the naked hand
His body bore his burning heart
That still on Florence strove to bring
God's fire for a burnt offering.
Even such was Dante's mood, when now,
Mocked for long years with Fortune's sport,
He dwelt at yet another court,
There where Verona's knee did bow
And her voice hailed with all acclaim
Can Grande della Scala's name.
As that lord's kingly guest awhile
His life we follow; through the days
Which walked in exile's barren ways,—
The nights which still beneath one smile
Heard through all spheres one song increase,—
"Even I, even I am Beatrice."
At Can La Scala's court, no doubt,
Due reverence did his steps attend;
The ushers on his path would bend
At ingoing as at going out;
The penmen waited on his call
At council-board, the grooms in hall.
And pages hushed their laughter down,
And gay squires stilled the merry stir,
When he passed up the dais-chamber
With set brows lordlier than a frown;
And tire-maids hidden among these
Drew close their loosened bodices.

Perhaps the priests, (exact to span
All God's circumference,) if at whiles
They found him wandering in their aisles,
Grudged ghostly greeting to the man
By whom, though not of ghostly guild,
With Heaven and Hell men's hearts were fill'd.
And the court-poets (he, forsooth,
A whole world's poet strayed to court!)
Had for his scorn their hate's retort.
He'd meet them flushed with easy youth,
Hot on their errands. Like noon-flies
They vexed him in the ears and eyes.
But at this court, peace still must wrench
Her chaplet from the teeth of war:
By day they held high watch afar,
At night they cried across the trench;
And still, in Dante's path, the fierce
Gaunt soldiers wrangled o'er their spears.
But vain seemed all the strength to him,
As golden convoys sunk at sea
Whose wealth might root out penury:
Because it was not, limb with limb,
Knit like his heart-strings round the wall
Of Florence, that ill pride might fall.
Yet in the tiltyard, when the dust
Cleared from the sundered press of knights
Ere yet again it swoops and smites,
He almost deemed his longing must
Find force to yield that multitude
And hurl that strength the way he would.
How should he move them,—fame and gain
On all hands calling them at strife?
He still might find but his one life
To give, by Florence counted vain;
One heart the false hearts made her doubt,
One voice she heard once and cast out.
Oh! if his Florence could but come,
A lily-sceptred damsel fair,
As her own Giotto painted her
On many shields and gates at home,—
A lady crowned, at a soft pace
Riding the lists round to the dais:
Till where Can Grande rules the lists,
As young as Truth, as calm as Force,
She draws her rein now, while her horse
Bows at the turn of the white wrists;
And when each knight within his stall
Gives ear, she speaks and tells them all:

All the foul tale,—truth sworn untrue
And falsehood's triumph. All the tale?
Great God! and must she not prevail
To fire them ere they heard it through,—
And hand achieve ere heart could rest
That high adventure of her quest?
How would his Florence lead them forth,
Her bridle ringing as she went;
And at the last within her tent,
'Neath golden lilies worship-worth,
How queenly would she bend the while
And thank the victors with her smile!
Also her lips should turn his way
And murmur: "O thou tried and true,
With whom I wept the long years through!
What shall it profit if I say,
Thee I remember? Nay, through thee
All ages shall remember me."
Peace, Dante, peace! The task is long,
The time wears short to compass it.
Within thine heart such hopes may flit
And find a voice in deathless song:
But lo! as children of man's earth,
Those hopes are dead before their birth.
Fame tells us that Verona's court
Was a fair place. The feet might still
Wander for ever at their will
In many ways of sweet resort;
And still in many a heart around
The Poet's name due honour found.
Watch we his steps. He comes upon
The women at their palm-playing.
The conduits round the gardens sing
And meet in scoops of milk-white stone,
Where wearied damsels rest and hold
Their hands in the wet spurt of gold.
One of whom, knowing well that he,
By some found stern, was mild with them,
Would run and pluck his garment's hem,
Saying, "Messer Dante, pardon me,"—
Praying that they might hear the song
Which first of all he made, when young.
"Donne che avete" . . . Thereunto
Thus would he murmur, having first
Drawn near the fountain, while she nurs'd
His hand against her side: a few
Sweet words, and scarcely those, half said:
Then turned, and changed, and bowed his head.

For then the voice said in his heart,
"Even I, even I am Beatrice";
And his whole life would yearn to cease:
Till having reached his room, apart
Beyond vast lengths of palace-floor,
He drew the arras round his door.
At such times, Dante, thou hast set
Thy forehead to the painted pane
Full oft, I know; and if the rain
Smote it outside, her fingers met
Thy brow; and if the sun fell there,
Her breath was on thy face and hair.
Then, weeping, I think certainly
Thou hast beheld, past sight of eyne,—
Within another room of thine
Where now thy body may not be
But where in thought thou still remain'st,—
A window often wept against:
The window thou, a youth, hast sought,
Flushed in the limpid eventime,
Ending with daylight the day's rhyme
Of her; where oftenwhiles her thought
Held thee—the lamp untrimmed to write—
In joy through the blue lapse of night.
At Can La Scala's court, no doubt,
Guests seldom wept. It was brave sport,
No doubt, at Can La Scala's court,
Within the palace and without;
Where music, set to madrigals,
Loitered all day through groves and halls.
Because Can Grande of his life
Had not had six-and-twenty years
As yet. And when the chroniclers
Tell you of that Vicenza strife
And of strifes elsewhere,—you must not
Conceive for church-sooth he had got
Just nothing in his wits but war:
Though doubtless 'twas the young man's joy
(Grown with his growth from a mere boy,)
To mark his "Viva Cane!" scare
The foe's shut front, till it would reel
All blind with shaken points of steel.
But there were places—held too sweet
For eyes that had not the due veil
Of lashes and clear lids—as well
In favour as his saddle-seat:
Breath of low speech he scorned not there
Nor light cool fingers in his hair.

Yet if the child whom the sire's plan
Made free of a deep treasure-chest
Scoffed it with ill-conditioned jest,—
We may be sure too that the man
Was not mere thews, nor all content
With lewdness swathed in sentiment.
So you may read and marvel not
That such a man as Dante—one
Who, while Can Grande's deeds were done,
Had drawn his robe round him and thought—
Now at the same guest-table far'd
Where keen Uguccio wiped his beard.
Through leaves and trellis-work the sun
Left the wine cool within the glass,—
They feasting where no sun could pass:
And when the women, all as one,
Rose up with brightened cheeks to go,
It was a comely thing, we know.
But Dante recked not of the wine;
Whether the women stayed or went,
His visage held one stern intent:
And when the music had its sign
To breathe upon them for more ease,
Sometimes he turned and bade it cease.
And as he spared not to rebuke
The mirth, so oft in council he
To bitter truth bore testimony:
And when the crafty balance shook
Well poised to make the wrong prevail,
Then Dante's hand would turn the scale.
And if some envoy from afar
Sailed to Verona's sovereign port
For aid or peace, and all the court
Fawned on its lord, "the Mars of war,
Sole arbiter of life and death,"—
Be sure that Dante saved his breath.
And Can La Scala marked askance
These things, accepting them for shame
And scorn, till Dante's guestship came
To be a peevish sufferance:
His host sought ways to make his days
Hateful; and such have many ways.
There was a Jester, a foul lout
Whom the court loved for graceless arts;
Sworn scholiast of the bestial parts
Of speech; a ribald mouth to shout
In Folly's horny tympanum
Such things as make the wise man dumb.

Much loved, him Dante loathed. And so,
One day when Dante felt perplexed
If any day that could come next
Were worth the waiting for or no,
And mute he sat amid their din,—
Can Grande called the Jester in.
Rank words, with such, are wit's best wealth.
Lords mouthed approval; ladies kept
Twittering with clustered heads, except
Some few that took their trains by stealth
And went. Can Grande shook his hair
And smote his thighs and laughed i' the air.
Then, facing on his guest, he cried,—
"Say, Messer Dante, how it is
I get out of a clown like this
More than your wisdom can provide."
And Dante: "'Tis man's ancient whim
That still his like seems good to him."
Also a tale is told, how once,
At clearing tables after meat,
Piled for a jest at Dante's feet
Were found the dinner's well-picked bones;
So laid, to please the banquet's lord,
By one who crouched beneath the board.
Then smiled Can Grande to the rest:—
"Our Dante's tuneful mouth indeed
Lacks not the gift on flesh to feed!"
"Fair host of mine," replied the guest,
"So many bones you'd not descry
If so it chanced the dog were I."
But wherefore should we turn the grout
In a drained cup, or be at strife
From the worn garment of a life
To rip the twisted ravel out?
Good needs expounding; but of ill
Each hath enough to guess his fill.
They named him Justicer-at-Law:
Each month to bear the tale in mind
Of hues a wench might wear unfin'd
And of the load an ox might draw;
To cavil in the weight of bread
And to see purse-thieves gibbeted.
And when his spirit wove the spell
(From under even to over-noon
In converse with itself alone,)
As high as Heaven, as low as Hell,—
He would be summoned and must go:
For had not Gian stabbed Giacomo?

Therefore the bread he had to eat
Seemed brackish, less like corn than tares;
And the rush-strown accustomed stairs
Each day were steeper to his feet;
And when the night-vigil was done,
His brows would ache to feel the sun.
Nevertheless, when from his kin
There came the tidings how at last
In Florence a decree was pass'd
Whereby all banished folk might win
Free pardon, so a fine were paid
And act of public penance made,—
This Dante writ in answer thus,
Words such as these: "That clearly they
In Florence must not have to say,—
The man abode aloof from us
Nigh fifteen years, yet lastly skulk'd
Hither to candleshrift and mulct.
"That he was one the Heavens forbid
To traffic in God's justice sold
By market-weight of earthly gold,
Or to bow down over the lid
Of steaming censers, and so be
Made clean of manhood's obloquy.
"That since no gate led, by God's will,
To Florence, but the one whereat
The priests and money-changers sat,
He still would wander; for that still,
Even through the body's prison-bars,
His soul possessed the sun and stars."
Such were his words. It is indeed
For ever well our singers should
Utter good words and know them good
Not through song only; with close heed
Lest, having spent for the work's sake
Six days, the man be left to make.
Months o'er Verona, till the feast
Was come for Florence the Free Town:
And at the shrine of Baptist John
The exiles, girt with many a priest
And carrying candles as they went,
Were held to mercy of the saint.
On the high seats in sober state,—
Gold neck-chains range o'er range below
Gold screen-work where the lilies grow,—
The Heads of the Republic sate,
Marking the humbled face go by
Each one of his house-enemy.

And as each proscript rose and stood
From kneeling in the ashen dust
On the shrine-steps, some magnate thrust
A beard into the velvet hood
Of his front colleague's gown, to see
The cinders stuck in the bare knee.
Tosinghi passed, Manelli passed,
Rinucci passed, each in his place;
But not an Alighieri's face
Went by that day from first to last
In the Republic's triumph; nor
A foot came home to Dante's door.
(RESPUBLICA—a public thing:
A shameful shameless prostitute,
Whose lust with one lord may not suit,
So takes by turn its revelling
A night with each, till each at morn
Is stripped and beaten forth forlorn,
And leaves her, cursing her. If she,
Indeed, have not some spice-draught, hid
In scent under a silver lid,
To drench his open throat with—he
Once hard asleep; and thrust him not
At dawn beneath the stairs to rot.
Such this Republic!—not the Maid
He yearned for; she who yet should stand
With Heaven's accepted hand in hand,
Invulnerable and unbetray'd:
To whom, even as to God, should be
Obeisance one with Liberty.)
Years filled out their twelve moons, and ceased
One in another; and alway
There were the whole twelve hours each day
And each night as the years increased;
And rising moon and setting sun
Beheld that Dante's work was done.
What of his work for Florence? Well
It was, he knew, and well must be.
Yet evermore her hate's decree
Dwelt in his thought intolerable:—
His body to be burned,—his soul
To beat its wings at hope's vain goal.
What of his work for Beatrice?
Now well-nigh was the third song writ,—
The stars a third time sealing it
With sudden music of pure peace:
For echoing thrice the threefold song,
The unnumbered stars the tone prolong.†

Each hour, as then the Vision pass'd,
He heard the utter harmony
Of the nine trembling spheres, till she
Bowed her eyes towards him in the last,
So that all ended with her eyes,
Hell, Purgatory, Paradise.
"It is my trust, as the years fall,
To write more worthily of her
Who now, being made God's minister,
Looks on His visage and knows all."
Such was the hope that love dar'd blend
With grief's slow fires, to make an end
Of the "New Life," his youth's dear book:
Adding thereunto: "In such trust
I labour, and believe I must
Accomplish this which my soul took
In charge, if God, my Lord and hers,
Leave my life with me a few years."
The trust which he had borne in youth
Was all at length accomplished. He
At length had written worthily—
Yea even of her; no rhymes uncouth
'Twixt tongue and tongue; but by God's aid
The first words Italy had said.
Ah! haply now the heavenly guide
Was not the last form seen by him:
But there that Beatrice stood slim
And bowed in passing at his side,
For whom in youth his heart made moan
Then when the city sat alone Quomodo sedet sola civitas!
—The words quoted by Dante in the Vita Nuova when
he speaks of the death of Beatrice.
Clearly herself: the same whom he
Met, not past girlhood, in the street,
Low-bosomed and with hidden feet;
And then as woman perfectly,
In years that followed, many an once,—
And now at last among the suns
In that high vision. But indeed
It may be memory might recall
Last to him then the first of all,—
The child his boyhood bore in heed
Nine years. At length the voice brought peace,—
"Even I, even I am Beatrice."
All this, being there, we had not seen.
Seen only was the shadow wrought
On the strong features bound in thought;
The vagueness gaining gait and mien;

The white streaks gathering clear to view
In the burnt beard the women knew.
For a tale tells that on his track,
As through Verona's streets he went,
This saying certain women sent:—
"Lo, he that strolls to Hell and back
At will! Behold him, how Hell's reek
Has crisped his beard and singed his cheek."
"Whereat" (Boccaccio's words) "he smiled
For pride in fame." It might be so:
Nevertheless we cannot know
If haply he were not beguiled
To bitterer mirth, who scarce could tell
If he indeed were back from Hell.
So the day came, after a space,
When Dante felt assured that there
The sunshine must lie sicklier
Even than in any other place,
Save only Florence. When that day
Had come, he rose and went his way.
He went and turned not. From his shoes
It may be that he shook the dust,
As every righteous dealer must
Once and again ere life can close:
And unaccomplished destiny
Struck cold his forehead, it may be.
No book keeps record how the Prince
Sunned himself out of Dante's reach,
Nor how the Jester stank in speech:
While courtiers, used to cringe and wince,
Poets and harlots, all the throng,
Let loose their scandal and their song.
No book keeps record if the seat
Which Dante held at his host's board
Were sat in next by clerk or lord,—
If leman lolled with dainty feet
At ease, or hostage brooded there,
Or priest lacked silence for his prayer.
Eat and wash hands, Can Grande;—scarce
We know their deeds now: hands which fed
Our Dante with that bitter bread;
And thou the watch-dog of those stairs
Which, of all paths his feet knew well,
Were steeper found than Heaven or Hell.

Tell me now in what hidden way is
Lady Flora the lovely Roman?
Where's Hipparchia, and where is Thais,
Neither of them the fairer woman?
Where is Echo, beheld of no man,
Only heard on river and mere—
She whose beauty was more than human?—
But where are the snows of yester-year?

Where's Heloise, the learned nun,
For whose sake Abeillard, I ween,
Lost manhood and put priesthood on?
(From Love he won such dule and teen!)
And where, I pray you, is the Queen
Who willed that Buridan should steer
Sewed in a sack's mouth down the Seine?—
But where are the snows of yester-year?

White Queen Blanche, like a queen of lilies,
With a voice like any mermaiden—
Bertha Broadfoot, Beatrice, Alice,
And Ermengarde the lady of Maine—
And that good Joan whom Englishmen
At Rouen doomed and burned her there—
Mother of God, where are they then?—
But where are the snows of yester-year?

Nay, never ask this week, fair lord,
Where they are gone, nor yet this year,
Except with this for an overword—
But where are the snows of yester-year?

Three Shadows

I looked and saw your eyes
In the shadow of your hair,
As a traveller sees the stream
In the shadow of the wood;
And I said, "My faint heart sighs,
Ah me! to linger there,
To drink deep and to dream
In that sweet solitude."
I looked and saw your heart
In the shadow of your eyes,
As a seeker sees the gold

In the shadow of the stream;
And I said, "Ah me! what art
Should win the immortal prize,
Whose want must make life cold
And Heaven a hollow dream?"
I looked and saw your love
In the shadow of your heart,
As a diver sees the pearl
In the shadow of the sea;
And I murmured, not above
My breath, but all apart,—
"Ah! you can love, true girl,
And is your love for me?"

The Orchard-Pit

Piled deep below the screening apple-branch
They lie with bitter apples in their hands:
And some are only ancient bones that blanch,
And some had ships that last year's wind did launch,
And some were yesterday the lords of lands.

In the soft dell, among the apple-trees,
High up above the hidden pit she stands,
And there for ever sings, who gave to these,
That lie below, her magic hour of ease,
And those her apples holden in their hands.

This in my dreams is shown me; and her hair
Crosses my lips and draws my burning breath;
Her song spreads golden wings upon the air,
Life's eyes are gleaming from her forehead fair,
And from her breasts the ravishing eyes of Death.

Men say to me that sleep hath many dreams,
Yet I knew never but this dream alone:
There, from a dried-up channel, once the stream's,
The glen slopes up; even such in sleep it seems
As to my waking sight the place well known.

My love I call her, and she loves me well:
But I love her as in the maelstrom's cup
The whirled stone loves the leaf inseparable
That clings to it round all the circling swell,
And that the same last eddy swallows up.

Ho ye that nothing have to lose! ho rouse ye, one and all!
Come from the sinks of the New Cut, the purlieus of Vauxhall!
Did ye not hear the mighty sound boom by ye as it went—
The Seven Dials strike the hour of man's enfranchisement?
Ho cock your eyes, my gallant pals, and swing your heavy staves:
Remember—Kings and Queens being out, the great cards will be Knaves.
And when the pack is ours—oh then at what a slapping pace
Shall the tens be trodden down to five, and the fives kicked down to ace!
It was but yesterday the Times and Post and Telegraph
Told how from France King Louy-Phil. was shaken out like chaff;
To-morrow, boys, the National, the Siècle, and the Débats,
Shall have to tell the self-same tale of "La Reine Victoria."
What! shall our incomes we've not got be taxed by puny John?
Shall the policeman keep Time back by bidding us move on?
Shall we too follow in the steps of that poor sneak Cochrane?
Shall it be said, "They came, they saw,—and bolted back again"?
Not so! albeit great men have been among us, and are floor'd—
(Frost, Williams, Jones, and other ones who now reside abroad)—
Among the master-spirits of the age there still are those
Who'll pick up fame—even though, when smelt, it makes men hold the nose.
What ho there! clear the way! make room for him, the "fly" and wise,
Who wrote in mystic grammar about London's "Mysteries,"—
For him who takes a proud delight to wallow in our kennels,—
For Mr. A. B. C. D. E. F. G. M. W. Reynolds!
Come, hoist him up! his pockets will afford convenient hold
To grab him by; and, if inside there silver is or gold,
And should it be found sticking to our hands when they're drawn out,
Why, 'twere a chance not fair to say ill-natured things about.
Silence! Hear, hear! He says that we're the sovereign people, we!
And now? And now he states the fact that one and one make three!
Now he makes casual mention of a certain Miscellany!
He says that he's the editor! He says it costs a penny!
O thou great Spirit of the World! shall not the lofty things
He saith be borne unto all time for noble lessonings?
Shall not our sons tell to their sons what we could do and dare
In this the great year Forty-eight and in Trafalgar Square?
Swathed in foul wood, yon column stood 'mid London's thousand marts;
And at their wine Committeemen grinned as they drank "The Arts":
But our good flint-stones have bowled down each poster-hidden board,
And from their hoarded malice our strong hands have stript the hoard.
Yon column is a prouder thing than Cæsar's triumph-arch!
It shall be called "The Column of the Glorious Days of March!"
And stonemasons' apprentices shall grow rich men therewith,
By contract-chiselling the names of Jones and Brown and Smith.

Upon what point of London, say, shall our next vengeance burst?
Shall the Exchange, or Parliament, be immolated first?
Which of the Squares shall we burn down?—which of the Palaces?
(The speaker is nailed by a policeman)
Oh please sir, don't! It isn't me. It's him. Oh don't, sir, please!

Wellington's Funeral

18th November 1852
"VICTORY!"
So once more the cry must be.
Duteous mourning we fulfil
In God's name; but by God's will,
Doubt not, the last word is still
"Victory!"
Funeral,
In the music round this pall,
Solemn grief yields earth to earth;
But what tones of solemn mirth
In the pageant of new birth
Rise and fall?
For indeed,
If our eyes were openèd,
Who shall say what escort floats
Here, which breath nor gleam denotes,—
Fiery horses, chariots
Fire-footed?
Trumpeter,
Even thy call he may not hear;
Long-known voice for ever past,
Till with one more trumpet-blast
God's assuring word at last
Reach his ear.
Multitude,
Hold your breath in reverent mood:
For while earth's whole kindred stand
Mute even thus on either hand,
This soul's labour shall be scann'd
And found good.
Cherubim,
Lift ye not even now your hymn?
Lo! once lent for human lack,
Michael's sword is rendered back.
Thrills not now the starry track,
Seraphim?
Gabriel,

Since the gift of thine "All hail!"
Out of Heaven no time hath brought
Gift with fuller blessing fraught
Than the peace which this man wrought
Passing well.
Be no word
Raised of bloodshed Christ-abhorr'd.
Say: "'Twas thus in His decrees
Who Himself, the Prince of Peace,
For His harvest's high increase
Sent a sword."
Veterans,
He by whom the neck of France
Then was given unto your heel,
Timely sought, may lend as well
To your sons his terrible
Countenance.
Waterloo!
As the last grave must renew,
Ere fresh death, the banshee-strain,—
So methinks upon thy plain
Falls some presage in the rain,
In the dew.
And O thou,
Watching, with an exile's brow
Unappeased, o'er death's dumb flood:—
Lo! the saving strength of God
In some new heart's English blood
Slumbers now.
Emperor,
Is this all thy work was for?—
Thus to see thy self-sought aim,
Yea thy titles, yea thy name,
In another's shame, to shame
Bandied o'er?
Thy great work is but begun.
With quick seed his end is rife
Whose long tale of conquering strife
Shows no triumph like his life
Lost and won.

In The Train, And at Versailles

In a dull swiftness we are carried by
With bodies left at sway and shaking knees.
The wind has ceased, or is a feeble breeze

Warm in the sun. The leaves are not yet dry
From yesterday's dense rain. All, low and high,
A strong green country; but, among its trees,
Ruddy and thin with Autumn. After these
There is the city still before the sky.
Versailles is reached. Pass we the galleries
And seek the gardens. A great silence here,
Through the long planted alleys, to the long
Distance of water. More than tune or song,
Silence shall grow to awe within thine eyes,
Till thy thought swim with the blue turning sphere.

On the Road to Waterloo: 17 October (En Vigilante, 2 Hours)

It is grey tingling azure overhead
With silver drift. Beneath, where from the green
The trees are reared, the distance stands between
At peace: and on this side the whole is spread
For sowing and for harvest, subjected
Clear to the sky and wind. The sun's slow height
Holds it through noon, and at the furthest night
It lies to the moist starshine and is fed.
Sometimes there is no country seen (for miles
You think) because of the near roadside path
Dense with long forest. Where the waters run
They have the sky sunk into them—a bath
Of still blue heat; and in their flow, at whiles,
There is a blinding vortex of the sun.

Antwerp and Bruges

I climbed the stair in Antwerp church,
What time the circling thews of sound
At sunset seem to heave it round.
Far up, the carillon did search
The wind, and the birds came to perch
Far under, where the gables wound.
In Antwerp harbour on the Scheldt
I stood along, a certain space
Of night. The mist was near my face;
Deep on, the flow was heard and felt.
The carillon kept pause, and dwelt
In music through the silent place.
John Memmeling and John van Eyck

Hold state at Bruges. In sore shame
I scanned the works that keep their name.
The carillon, which then did strike
Mine ears, was heard of theirs alike:
It set me closer unto them.
I climbed at Bruges all the flight
The belfry has of ancient stone.
For leagues I saw the east wind blown;
The earth was grey, the sky was white.
I stood so near upon the height
That my flesh felt the carillon.

At the Station of the Versailles Railway

I waited for the train unto Versailles.
I hung with bonnes and gamins on the bridge
Watching the gravelled road where, ridge with ridge,
Under black arches gleam the iron rails
Clear in the darkness, till the darkness fails
And they press on to light again—again
To reach the dark. I waited for the train
Unto Versailles; I leaned over the bridge,
And wondered, cold and drowsy, why the knave
Claude is in worship; and why (sense apart)
Rubens preferred a mustard vehicle.
The wind veered short. I turned upon my heel
Saying, "Correggio was a toad"; then gave
Three dizzy yawns, and knew not of the Art.

Between Ghent and Bruges

Ah yes, exactly so; but when a man
Has trundled out of England into France
And half through Belgium, always in this prance
Of steam, and still has stuck to his first plan—
Blank verse or sonnets; and as he began
Would end;—why, even the blankest verse may chance
To falter in default of circumstance,
And even the sonnet miss its mystic span.
Trees will be trees, grass grass, pools merely pools,
Unto the end of time and Belgium—points
Of fact which Poets (very abject fools)
Get scent of—once their epithets grown tame
And scarce. Even to these foreign rails—my joints

Begin to find their jolting much the same.

L'envoi: Brussels, Hotel Du Midi

It's copied out at last: very poor stuff
Writ in the cold, with pauses of the cramp.
Direct, dear William, to the Poste Restante
At Ghent—here written Gand—Gong, Huntice.
We go to Antwerp first, but shall not stay;
After, to Ghent and Bruges; and after that
To Ostend, and thence home. To Waterloo
Was yesterday. Thither, and there, and back,
I managed to scrawl something,—most of it
Bad, and the sonnet at the close mere slosh.
'Twas only made because I was knocked up,
And it helped yawning. Take it, and the rest.

At the Sunrise, 1848

God said, Let there be light; and there was light.
Then heard we sounds as though the Earth did sing
And the Earth's angel cried upon the wing:
We saw priests fall together and turn white:
And covered in the dust from the sun's sight,
A king was spied, and yet another king.
We said: "The round world keeps its balancing;
On this globe, they and we are opposite,—
If it is day with us, with them 'tis night."
Still, Man, in thy just pride, remember this:—
Thou hadst not made that thy sons' sons shall ask
What the word king may mean in their day's task,
But for the light that led: and if light is,
It is because God said, Let there be light.

Sunset Wings

To-night this sunset spreads two golden wings
Cleaving the western sky;
Winged too with wind it is, and winnowings
Of birds; as if the day's last hour in rings
Of strenuous flight must die.
Sun-steeped in fire, the homeward pinions sway

Above the dovecote-tops;
And clouds of starlings, ere they rest with day,
Sink, clamorous like mill-waters, at wild play,
By turns in every copse:
Each tree heart-deep the wrangling rout receives,—
Save for the whirr within,
You could not tell the starlings from the leaves;
Then one great puff of wings, and the swarm heaves
Away with all its din.
Even thus Hope's hours, in ever-eddying flight,
To many a refuge tend;
With the first light she laughed, and the last light
Glows round her still; who natheless in the night
At length must make an end.
And now the mustering rooks innumerable
Together sail and soar,
While for the day's death, like a tolling knell,
Unto the heart they seem to cry, Farewell,
No more, farewell, no more!
Is Hope not plumed, as 'twere a fiery dart?
And oh! thou dying day,
Even as thou goest must she too depart,
And Sorrow fold such pinions on the heart
As will not fly away?

English May

Would God your health were as this month of May
Should be, were this not England,—and your face
Abroad, to give the gracious sunshine grace
And laugh beneath the budding hawthorn-spray.
But here the hedgerows pine from green to grey
While yet May's lyre is tuning, and her song
Is weak in shade that should in sun be strong;
And your pulse springs not to so faint a lay.
If in my life be breath of Italy,
Would God that I might yield it all to you!
So, when such grafted warmth had burgeoned through
The languor of your Maytime's hawthorn-tree,
My spirit at rest should walk unseen and see
The garland of your beauty bloom anew.

A Little While

A little while a little love
The hour yet bears for thee and me
Who have not drawn the veil to see
If still our heaven be lit above
Thou merely, at the day's last sigh,
Hast felt thy soul prolong the tone;
And I have heard the night-wind cry
And deem'd its speech mine own.

A little while a little love
The scattering autumn hoards for us
Whose bower is not yet ruinous
Nor quite unleav'd our songless grove.
Only across the shaken boughs
We hear the flood-tides seek the sea,
And deep in both our hearts they rouse
One wail for thee and me.

A little while a little love
May yet be ours who have not said
The word it makes our eyes afraid
To know that each is thinking of.
Not yet the end: be our lips dumb
In smiles a little season yet:
I 'll tell thee, when the end is come,
How we may best forget.

The Sin of Detection

She bowed her face among them all, as one
By one they rose and went. A little scorn
They showed—a very little. More forlorn
She seemed because of that: she might have grown
Proud else in her turn, and have so made known
What she well knew—that the free—hearted corn,
Kissed by the hot air freely all the morn,
Is better than the weed which has its own
Foul glut in secret. Both her white breasts heaved
Like heaving water with their weight of lace;
And her long tresses, full of musk and myrrh,
Were shaken from the braids her fingers weaved,
So that they hid the shame in her pale face.
Then I stept forth, and bowed addressing her.

O Lady amorous,
Merciless lady,
Full blithely play'd ye
These your beguilings.
So with an urchin
A man makes merry,—
In mirth grows clamorous,
Laughs and rejoices,—
But when his choice is
To fall aweary,
Cheats him with silence.
This is Love's portion:—
In much wayfaring
With many burdens
He loads his servants,
But at the sharing,
The underservice
And overservice
Are alike barren.

As my disaster
Your jest I cherish,
And well may perish.
Even so a falcon
Is sometimes taken
And scantly cautell'd;
Till when his master
At length to loose him,
To train and use him,
Is after all gone,—
The creature's throttled
And will not waken.
Wherefore, my lady,
If you will own me,
O look upon me!
If I'm not thought on,
At least perceive me!
O do not leave me
So much forgotten!

If, lady, truly
You wish my profit,
What follows of it
Though still you say so?—
For all your well-wishes
I still am waiting.

I grow unruly,
And deem at last I'm
Only your pastime.
A child will play so,
Who greatly relishes
Sporting and petting
With a little wild bird:
Unaware he kills it,—
Then turns it, feels it,
Calls it with a mild word,
Is angry after,—
Then again in laughter
Loud is the child heard.

O my delightful
My own my lady,
Upon the Mayday
Which brought me to you
Was all my haste then
But a fool's venture?
To have my sight full
Of you propitious
Truly my wish was,
And to pursue you
And let love chasten
My heart to the centre.
But warming, lady,
May end in burning.
Of all this yearning
What comes, I beg you?
In all your glances
What is't a man sees?—
Fever and ague.

Ladies That Have Intelligence in Love

Ladies that have intelligence in love,
Of mine own lady I would speak with you;
Not that I hope to count her praises through,
But telling what I may, to ease my mind.
And I declare that when I speak thereof,
Love sheds such perfect sweetness over me
That if my courage failed not, certainly
To him my listeners must be all resign'd
Wherefore I will not speak in such large kind
That mine own speech should foil me, which were base;

But only will discourse of her high grace
In these poor words, the best that I can find,
With you alone, dear dames and damozels:
'Twere ill to speak thereof with any else.

An angel, of his blessed knowledge, saith
To God: 'Lord, in the world that Thou hast made,
A miracle in action is display'd,
By reason of a soul whose splendors fare
Even hither: and since Heaven requireth
Nought saving her, for her it prayeth Thee,
Thy Saints crying aloud continually.'
Yet Pity still defends our earthly share
In that sweet soul; God answering thus the prayer:
'My well-belovèd, suffer that in peace
Your hope remain, while so My pleasure is,
There where one dwells who dreads the loss of her:
And who in Hell unto the doomed shall say,
'I have looked on that for which God's chosen pray.''

My lady is desired in the high Heaven:
Wherefore, it now behoveth me to tell,
Saying: Let any maid that would be well
Esteemed keep with her: for as she goes by,
Into foul hearts a deathly chill is driven
By Love, that makes ill thought to perish there:
While any who endures to gaze on her
Must either be ennobled, or else die.
When one deserving to be raised so high
Is found, 'tis then her power attains its proof,
Making his heart strong for his soul's behoof
With the full strength of meek humility.
Also this virtue owns she, by God's will:
Who speaks with her can never come to ill.

Love saith concerning her: 'How chanceth it
That flesh, which is of dust, should be thus pure?'
Then, gazing always, he makes oath: 'Forsure,
This is a creature of God till now unknown.'
She hath that paleness of the pearl that's fit
In a fair woman, so much and not more;
She is as high as Nature's skill can soar;
Beauty is tried by her comparison.
Whatever her sweet eyes are turned upon,
Spirits of love do issue thence in flame,
Which through their eyes who then may look on them
Pierce to the heart's deep chamber every one.
And in her smile Love's image you may see;

Whence none can gaze upon her steadfastly.

Dear Song, I know thou wilt hold gentle speech
With many ladies, when I send thee forth:
Wherefore (being mindful that thou hadst thy birth)
From Love, and art a modest, simple child,)
Whomso thou meetest, say thou this to each:
'Give me good speed! To her I wend along
In whose much strength my weakness is made strong.'
And if, i' the end, thou wouldst not be beguiled
Of all thy labor seek not the defiled
And common sort; but rather choose to be
Where man and woman dwell in courtesy.
So to the road thou shalt be reconciled,
And find the Lady, and with the lady, Love.
Commend thou me to each, as doth behove.

First Love Remembered

Peace in her chamber, wheresoe'er
It be, a holy place:
The thought still brings my soul such grace
As morning meadows wear.
Whether it still be small and light,
A maid's who dreams alone,
As from her orchard-gate the moon
Its ceiling showed at night:
Or whether, in a shadow dense
As nuptial hymns invoke,
Innocent maidenhood awoke
To married innocence:
There still the thanks unheard await
The unconscious gift bequeathed:
For there my soul this hour has breathed
An air inviolate.

Genius in Beauty

Beauty like hers is genius. Not the call
Of Homer's or of Dante's heart sublime,—
Not Michael's hand furrowing the zones of time,—
Is more with compassed mysteries musical;
Nay, not in Spring's Summer's sweet footfall
More gathered gifts exuberant Life bequeaths

Than doth this sovereign face, whose love-spell breathes
Even from its shadowed contour on the wall.

As many men are poets in their youth,
But for one sweet-strung soul the wires prolong
Even through all change the indomitable song;
So in likewise the envenomed years, whose tooth
Rends shallower grace with ruin void of truth,
Upon this beauty's power shall wreak no wrong.

Our Lady of the Rocks by Leonardo da Vinci

Mother, is this the darkness of the end,
The Shadow of Death? and is that outer sea
Infinite imminent Eternity?
And does the death-pang by man's seed sustained
In Time's each instant cause thy face to bend
Its silent prayer upon the Son, while He
Blesses the dead with His hand silently
To His long day which hours no more offend?
Mother of grace, the pass is difficult,
Keen as these rocks, and the bewildered souls
Throng it like echoes, blindly shuddering through.
Thy name, O Lord, each spirit's voice extols,
Whose peace abides in the dark avenue
Amid the bitterness of things occult.

The Portrait

This is her picture as she was:
It seems a thing to wonder on,
As though mine image in the glass
Should tarry when myself am gone.
I gaze until she seems to stir,—
Until mine eyes almost aver
That now, even now, the sweet lips part
To breathe the words of the sweet heart:—
And yet the earth is over her.

Alas! even such the thin-drawn ray
That makes the prison-depths more rude,—
The drip of water night and day
Giving a tongue to solitude.
Yet only this, of love's whole prize,

Remains; save what in mournful guise
Takes counsel with my soul alone,—
Save what is secret and unknown,
Below the earth, above the skies.

In painting her I shrin'd her face
Mid mystic trees, where light falls in
Hardly at all; a covert place
Where you might think to find a din
Of doubtful talk, and a live flame
Wandering, and many a shape whose name
Not itself knoweth, and old dew,
And your own footsteps meeting you,
And all things going as they came.

A deep dim wood; and there she stands
As in that wood that day: for so
Was the still movement of her hands
And such the pure line's gracious flow.
And passing fair the type must seem,
Unknown the presence and the dream.
'Tis she: though of herself, alas!
Less than her shadow on the grass
Or than her image in the stream.

That day we met there, I and she
One with the other all alone;
And we were blithe; yet memory
Saddens those hours, as when the moon
Looks upon daylight. And with her
I stoop'd to drink the spring-water,
Athirst where other waters sprang;
And where the echo is, she sang,—
My soul another echo there.

But when that hour my soul won strength
For words whose silence wastes and kills,
Dull raindrops smote us, and at length
Thunder'd the heat within the hills.
That eve I spoke those words again
Beside the pelted window-pane;
And there she hearken'd what I said,
With under-glances that survey'd
The empty pastures blind with rain.

Next day the memories of these things,
Like leaves through which a bird has flown,
Still vibrated with Love's warm wings;

Till I must make them all my own
And paint this picture. So, 'twixt ease
Of talk and sweet long silences,
She stood among the plants in bloom
At windows of a summer room,
To feign the shadow of the trees.

And as I wrought, while all above
And all around was fragrant air,
In the sick burthen of my love
It seem'd each sun-thrill'd blossom there
Beat like a heart among the leaves.
O heart that never beats nor heaves,
In that one darkness lying still,
What now to thee my love's great will
Or the fine web the sunshine weaves?

For now doth daylight disavow
Those days,—nought left to see or hear.
Only in solemn whispers now
At night-time these things reach mine ear;
When the leaf-shadows at a breath
Shrink in the road, and all the heath,
Forest and water, far and wide,
In limpid starlight glorified,
Lie like the mystery of death.

Last night at last I could have slept,
And yet delay'd my sleep till dawn,
Still wandering. Then it was I wept:
For unawares I came upon
Those glades where once she walk'd with me:
And as I stood there suddenly,
All wan with traversing the night,
Upon the desolate verge of light
Yearn'd loud the iron-bosom'd sea.

Even so, where Heaven holds breath and hears
The beating heart of Love's own breast,—
Where round the secret of all spheres
All angels lay their wings to rest,—
How shall my soul stand rapt and aw'd,
When, by the new birth borne abroad
Throughout the music of the suns,
It enters in her soul at once
And knows the silence there for God!

Here with her face doth memory sit

Meanwhile, and wait the day's decline,
Till other eyes shall look from it,
Eyes of the spirit's Palestine,
Even than the old gaze tenderer:
While hopes and aims long lost with her
Stand round her image side by side,
Like tombs of pilgrims that have died
About the Holy Sepulchre.

Joan of Arc

This word had Merlin said from of old:—
That out of the Oak Tree Shade
In the day of France's direst dule,
God's hand should send a Maid.
And where Domremy, by Burgundy,
Sits crowned with its oakenshaw,
Even there Joan d'Arc, the Maid of God's Ark,
The light of the day first saw.

Where spirits go, what man may know?
Yet this may of man be said:—
That, when Time is o'er and all hath sufficed,
Shall the world's chief Christ-fire rise to Christ
From the ashes of Joan the Maid.

Vox Ecclesiae, Vox Christi

Not 'neath the altar only,—yet, in sooth,
There more than elsewhere,—is the cry, "How long?"
The right sown there hath still borne fruit in wrong—
The wrong waxed fourfold. Thence, (in hate of truth)
O'er weapons blessed for carnage, to fierce youth
From evil age, the word hath hissed along:—
"Ye are the Lord's: go forth, destroy, be strong:
Christ's Church absolves ye from Christ's law of ruth."
Therefore the wine-cup at the altar is
As Christ's own blood indeed, and as the blood
Of Christ's elect, at divers seasons spilt
On the altar-stone, that to man's church, for this,
Shall prove a stone of stumbling,—whence it stood
To be rent up ere the true Church be built.

After the French Liberation of Italy

As when the last of the paid joys of love
Has come and gone; and with a single kiss
At length, and with one laugh of satiate bliss,
The wearied man a minute rests above
The wearied woman, no more urged to move
In those long throes of longing, till they glide,
Now lightlier clasped, each to the other's side,
In joys past acting, not past dreaming of:—
So Europe now beneath this paramour
Lies for a little out of use,—full oft
Submissive to his lust, a loveless whore.
He wakes, she sleeps, the breath falls slow and soft.
Wait: the bought body holds a birth within,
An harlot's child, to scourge her for her sin.

After the German Subjugation of France, 1871

Lo the twelfth year—the wedding-feast come round
With years for months—and lo the babe new-born;
Out of the womb's rank furnace cast forlorn,
And with contagious effluence seamed and crown'd.
To hail this birth, what fiery tongues surround
Hell's Pentecost—what clamour of all cries
That swell, from Absalom's scoff to Shimei's,
One scornful gamut of tumultuous sound!
For now the harlot's heart on a new sleeve
Is prankt; and her heart's lord of yesterday
(Spurned from her bed, whose worm-spun silks o'erlay
Such fretwork as that other worm can weave)
Takes in his ears the vanished world's last yell,
And in his flesh the closing teeth of Hell.

The White Ship Henry I of England—25th November 1120

By none but me can the tale be told,
The butcher of Rouen, poor Berold.
(Lands are swayed by a King on a throne.)
'Twas a royal train put forth to sea,
Yet the tale can be told by none but me.
(The sea hath no King but God alone.)
King Henry held it as life's whole gain

That after his death his son should reign.
`Twas so in my youth I heard men say,
And my old age calls it back to-day.
King Henry of England's realm was he,
And Henry Duke of Normandy.
The times had changed when on either coast
"Clerkly Harry" was all his boast.
Of ruthless strokes full many an one
He had struck to crown himself and his son;
And his elder brother's eyes were gone.
And when to the chase his court would crowd,
The poor flung ploughshares on his road,
And shrieked: "Our cry is from King to God!"
But all the chiefs of the English land
Had knelt and kissed the Prince's hand.
And next with his son he sailed to France
To claim the Norman allegiance:
And every baron in Normandy
Had taken the oath of fealty.
'Twas sworn and sealed, and the day had come
When the King and the Prince might journey home:
For Christmas cheer is to home hearts dear,
And Christmas now was drawing near.
Stout Fitz-Stephen came to the King,—
A pilot famous in seafaring;
And he held to the King, in all men's sight,
A mark of gold for his tribute's right.
"Liege Lord! my father guided the ship
From whose boat your father's foot did slip
When he caught the English soil in his grip,
"And cried: 'By this clasp I claim command
O'er every rood of English land!'
"He was borne to the realm you rule o'er now
In that ship with the archer carved at her prow:
"And thither I'll bear, an it be my due,
Your father's son and his grandson too.
"The famed White Ship is mine in the bay;
From Harfleur's harbour she sails to-day,
"With masts fair-pennoned as Norman spears
And with fifty well-tried mariners."
Quoth the King: "My ships are chosen each one,
But I'll not say nay to Stephen's son.
"My son and daughter and fellowship
Shall cross the water in the White Ship."
The King set sail with the eve's south wind,
And soon he left that coast behind.
The Prince and all his, a princely show,
Remained in the good White Ship to go.

With noble knights and with ladies fair,
With courtiers and sailors gathered there,
Three hundred living souls we were:
And I Berold was the meanest hind
In all that train to the Prince assign'd.
The Prince was a lawless shameless youth;
From his father's loins he sprang without ruth:
Eighteen years till then he had seen,
And the devil's dues in him were eighteen.
And now he cried: "Bring wine from below;
Let the sailors revel ere yet they row:
"Our speed shall o'ertake my father's flight
Though we sail from the harbour at midnight."
The rowers made good cheer without check;
The lords and ladies obeyed his beck;
The night was light, and they danced on the deck.
But at midnight's stroke they cleared the bay,
And the White Ship furrowed the water-way.
The sails were set, and the oars kept tune
To the double flight of the ship and the moon:
Swifter and swifter the White Ship sped
Till she flew as the spirit flies from the dead:
As white as a lily glimmered she
Like a ship's fair ghost upon the sea.
And the Prince cried, "Friends, 'tis the hour to sing!
Is a songbird's course so swift on the wing?"
And under the winter stars' still throng,
From brown throats, white throats, merry and strong,
The knights and the ladies raised a song.
A song,—nay, a shriek that rent the sky,
That leaped o'er the deep!—the grievous cry
Of three hundred living that now must die.
An instant shriek that sprang to the shock
As the ship's keel felt the sunken rock.
'Tis said that afar—a shrill strange sigh—
The King's ships heard it and knew not why.
Pale Fitz-Stephen stood by the helm
'Mid all those folk that the waves must whelm.
A great King's heir for the waves to whelm,
And the helpless pilot pale at the helm!
The ship was eager and sucked athirst,
By the stealthy stab of the sharp reef pierc'd:
And like the moil round a sinking cup
The waters against her crowded up.
A moment the pilot's senses spin,—
The next he snatched the Prince 'mid the din,
Cut the boat loose, and the youth leaped in.
A few friends leaped with him, standing near.

"Row! the sea's smooth and the night is clear!"
"What! none to be saved but these and I?"
"Row, row as you'd live! All here must die!"
Out of the churn of the choking ship,
Which the gulf grapples and the waves strip,
They struck with the strained oars' flash and dip.
'Twas then o'er the splitting bulwarks' brim
The Prince's sister screamed to him.
He gazed aloft, still rowing apace,
And through the whirled surf he knew her face.
To the toppling decks clave one and all
As a fly cleaves to a chamber-wall.
I Berold was clinging anear;
I prayed for myself and quaked with fear,
But I saw his eyes as he looked at her.
He knew her face and he heard her cry,
And he said, "Put back! she must not die!"
And back with the current's force they reel
Like a leaf that's drawn to a water-wheel.
'Neath the ship's travail they scarce might float,
But he rose and stood in the rocking boat.
Low the poor ship leaned on the tide:
O'er the naked keel as she best might slide,
The sister toiled to the brother's side.
He reached an oar to her from below,
And stiffened his arms to clutch her so.
But now from the ship some spied the boat,
And "Saved!" was the cry from many a throat.
And down to the boat they leaped and fell:
It turned as a bucket turns in a well,
And nothing was there but the surge and swell.
The Prince that was and the King to come,
There in an instant gone to his doom,
Despite of all England's bended knee
And maugre the Norman fealty!
He was a Prince of lust and pride;
He showed no grace till the hour he died.
When he should be King, he oft would vow,
He'd yoke the peasant to his own plough.
O'er him the ships score their furrows now.
God only knows where his soul did wake,
But I saw him die for his sister's sake.
By none but me can the tale be told,
The butcher of Rouen, poor Berold.
(Lands are swayed by a King on a throne.)
'Twas a royal train put forth to sea,
Yet the tale can be told by none but me.
(The sea hath no King but God alone.)

And now the end came o'er the waters' womb
Like the last great Day that's yet to come.
With prayers in vain and curses in vain,
The White Ship sundered on the mid-main:
And what were men and what was a ship
Were toys and splinters in the sea's grip.
I Berold was down in the sea;
And passing strange though the thing may be,
Of dreams then known I remember me.
Blithe is the shout on Harfleur's strand
When morning lights the sails to land:
And blithe is Honfleur's echoing gloam
When mothers call the children home:
And high do the bells of Rouen beat
When the Body of Christ goes down the street.
These things and the like were heard and shown
In a moment's trance 'neath the sea alone;
And when I rose, 'twas the sea did seem,
And not these things, to be all a dream.
The ship was gone and the crowd was gone,
And the deep shuddered and the moon shone,
And in a strait grasp my arms did span
The mainyard rent from the mast where it ran;
And on it with me was another man.
Where lands were none 'neath the dim sea-sky,
We told our names, that man and I.
"O I am Godefroy de l'Aigle hight,
And son I am to a belted knight."
"And I am Berold the butcher's son
Who slays the beasts in Rouen town."
Then cried we upon God's name, as we
Did drift on the bitter winter sea.
But lo! a third man rose o'er the wave,
And we said, "Thank God! us three may He save!"
He clutched to the yard with panting stare,
And we looked and knew Fitz-Stephen there.
He clung, and "What of the Prince?" quoth he.
"Lost, lost!" we cried. He cried, "Woe on me!"
And loosed his hold and sank through the sea.
And soul with soul again in that space
We two were together face to face:
And each knew each, as the moments sped,
Less for one living than for one dead:
And every still star overhead
Seemed an eye that knew we were but dead.
And the hours passed; till the noble's son
Sighed, "God be thy help! my strength's foredone!
"O farewell, friend, for I can no more!"

"Christ take thee!" I moaned; and his life was o'er.
Three hundred souls were all lost but one,
And I drifted over the sea alone.
At last the morning rose on the sea
Like an angel's wing that beat tow'rds me.
Sore numbed I was in my sheepskin coat;
Half dead I hung, and might nothing note,
Till I woke sun-warmed in a fisher-boat.
The sun was high o'er the eastern brim
As I praised God and gave thanks to Him.
That day I told my tale to a priest,
Who charged me, till the shrift were releas'd,
That I should keep it in mine own breast.
And with the priest I thence did fare
To King Henry's court at Winchester.
We spoke with the King's high chamberlain,
And he wept and mourned again and again,
As if his own son had been slain:
And round us ever there crowded fast
Great men with faces all aghast:
And who so bold that might tell the thing
Which now they knew to their lord the King?
Much woe I learnt in their communing.
The King had watched with a heart sore stirred
For two whole days, and this was the third:
And still to all his court would he say,
"What keeps my son so long away?"
And they said: "The ports lie far and wide
That skirt the swell of the English tide;
"And England's cliffs are not more white
Than her women are, and scarce so light
Her skies as their eyes are blue and bright;
"And in some port that he reached from France
The Prince has lingered for his pleasaùnce."
But once the King asked: "What distant cry
Was that we heard 'twixt the sea and sky?"
And one said: "With suchlike shouts, pardie!
Do the fishers fling their nets at sea."
And one: "Who knows not the shrieking quest
When the sea-mew misses its young from the nest?"
'Twas thus till now they had soothed his dread,
Albeit they knew not what they said:
But who should speak to-day of the thing
That all knew there except the King?
Then pondering much they found a way,
And met round the King's high seat that day:
And the King sat with a heart sore stirred,
And seldom he spoke and seldom heard.

'Twas then through the hall the King was 'ware
Of a little boy with golden hair,
As bright as the golden poppy is
That the beach breeds for the surf to kiss:
Yet pale his cheek as the thorn in Spring,
And his garb black like the raven's wing.
Nothing heard but his foot through the hall,
For now the lords were silent all.
And the King wondered, and said, "Alack!
Who sends me a fair boy dressed in black?
"Why, sweet heart, do you pace through the hall
As though my court were a funeral?"
Then lowly knelt the child at the dais,
And looked up weeping in the King's face.
"O wherefore black, O King, ye may say,
For white is the hue of death to-day.
"Your son and all his fellowship
Lie low in the sea with the White Ship."
King Henry fell as a man struck dead;
And speechless still he stared from his bed
When to him next day my rede I read.
There's many an hour must needs beguile
A King's high heart that he should smile,—
Full many a lordly hour, full fain
Of his realm's rule and pride of his reign:—
But this King never smiled again.
By none but me can the tale be told,
The butcher of Rouen, poor Berold.
(Lands are swayed by a King on a throne.)
'Twas a royal train put forth to sea,
Yet the tale can be told by none but me.
(The sea hath no King but God alone.)

On Refusal of Aid Between Nations

Not that the earth is changing, O my God!
Nor that the seasons totter in their walk,—
Not that the virulent ill of act and talk
Seethes ever as a winepress ever trod,—
Not therefore are we certain that the rod
Weighs in thine hand to smite thy world; though now
Beneath thine hand so many nations bow,
So many kings:—not therefore, O my God!—
But because Man is parcelled out in men
To-day; because, for any wrongful blow
No man not stricken asks, "I would be told

Why thou dost thus;" but his heart whispers then,
"He is he, I am I." By this we know
That our earth falls asunder, being old.

Words on the Window Pane

Did she in summer write it, or in spring,
Or with this wail of autumn at her ears,
Or in some winter left among old years
Scratched it through tettered cark? A certain thing
That round her heart the frost was hardening,
Not to be thawed of tears, which on this pane
Channelled the rime, perchance, in fevered rain,
For false man's sake and love's most bitter sting.
Howbeit, between this last word and the next
Unwritten, subtly seasoned was the smart,
And here at least the grace to weep: if she,
Rather, midway in her disconsolate text,
Rebelled not, loathing from the trodden heart
That thing which she had found man's love to be.

Parted Presence

Love, I speak to your heart,
Your heart that is always here.
Oh draw me deep to its sphere,
Though you and I are apart,
And yield, by the spirit's art,
Each distant gift that is dear.
O love, my love, you are here!
Your eyes are afar to-day,
Yet, love, look now in mine eyes.
Two hearts sent forth may despise
All dead things by the way.
All between is decay,
Dead hours and this hour that dies.
O love, look deep in mine eyes!
Your hands to-day are not here,
Yet lay them, love, in my hands.
The hourglass sheds its sands
All day for the dead hours' bier;
But now, as two hearts draw near,
This hour like a flower expands.
O love, your hands in my hands!

Your voice is not on the air,
Yet, love, I can hear your voice:
It bids my heart to rejoice
As knowing your heart is there,—
A music sweet to declare
The truth of your steadfast choice.
O love, how sweet is your voice!
To-day your lips are afar,
Yet draw my lips to them, love.
Around, beneath, and above,
Is frost to bind and to bar;
But where I am and you are,
Desire and the fire thereof.
O kiss me, kiss me, my love!
Your heart is never away,
But ever with mine, for ever,
For ever without endeavour,
To-morrow, love, as to-day;
Two blent hearts never astray,
Two souls no power may sever,
Together, O my love, for ever!

Sacrament Hymn

On a fair Sabbath day, when His banquet is spread,
It is pleasant to feast with my Lord:
His stewards stand robed at the foot and the head
Of the soul-filling, life-giving board.
All the guests here had burthens; but by the King's grant
We left them behind when we came;
The burthen of wealth and the burthen of want,
And even the burthen of shame.
And oh, when we take them again at the gate,
Though still we must bear them awhile,
Much smaller they'll seem in the lane that grows strait,
And much lighter to lift at the stile.
For that which is in us is life to the heart,
Is dew to the soles of the feet,
Fresh strength to the loins, giving ease from their smart,
Warmth in frost, and a breeze in the heat.
No feast where the belly alone hath its fill,—
He gives me His body and blood;
The blood and the body (I'll think of it still)
Of my Lord, which is Christ, which is God.

Chimes

I

Honey-flowers to the honey-comb,
And the honey-bee's from home.
A honey-comb and a honey-flower,
And the bee shall have his hour.
A honeyed heart for the honey-comb,
And the humming bee flies home.
A heavy heart in the honey-flower,
And the bee has had his hour.

II

A honey-cell's in the honeysuckle,
And the honey-bee knows it well.
The honey-comb has a heart of honey,
And the humming bee's so bonny.
A honey-flower's the honeysuckle,
And the bee's in the honey-bell.
The honeysuckle is sucked of honey,
And the bee is heavy and bonny.

III

Brown shell first for the butterfly,
And a bright wing by and by.
Butterfly, good-bye to your shell,
And, bright wings, speed you well.
Bright lamplight for the butterfly
And a burnt wing by and by.
Butterfly, alas for your shell,
And, bright wings, fare you well.

IV

Lost love-labour and lullaby,
And lowly let love lie.
Lost love-morrow and love fellow
And love's life lying low.
Lovelorn labour and life laid by,
And lowly let love lie.
Late love-longing and life-sorrow
And love's life lying low.

V

Beauty's body and benison
With a bosom-flower new-blown.
Bitter beauty and blessing bann'd
With a breast to burn and brand.

Beauty's bower in the dust o'erblown
With a bare white breast of bone.
Barren beauty and bower of sand
With a blast on either hand.

VI

Buried bars in the breakwater
And bubble of the brimming weir.
Body's blood in the breakwater
And a buried body's bier.
Buried bones in the breakwater
And bubble of the brawling weir.
Bitter tears in the breakwater
And a breaking heart to bear.

VII

Hollow heaven and the hurricane
And hurry of the heavy rain.
Hurried clouds in the hollow heaven
And a heavy rain hard-driven.
The heavy rain it hurries amain
And heaven and the hurricane.
Hurrying wind o'er the heaven's hollow
And the heavy rain to follow.

Venus Verticordia (For A Picture)

She hath the apple in her hand for thee,
Yet almost in her heart would hold it back;
She muses, with her eyes upon the track
Of that which in thy spirit they can see.
Haply, "Behold, he is at peace," saith she;
"Alas! the apple for his lips,—the dart
That follows its brief sweetness to his heart,—
The wandering of his feet perpetually!"
A little space her glance is still and coy;
But if she give the fruit that works her spell,
Those eyes shall flame as for her Phrygian boy.
Then shall her bird's strained throat the woe foretell,
And her far seas moan as a single shell,
Pandora (For a Picture)
What of the end, Pandora? Was it thine,
The deed that set these fiery pinions free?
Ah! wherefore did the Olympian consistory
In its own likeness make thee half divine?
Was it that Juno's brow might stand a sign

For ever? and the mien of Pallas be
A deadly thing? and that all men might see
In Venus' eyes the gaze of Proserpine?
What of the end? These beat their wings at will,
The ill-born things, the good things turned to ill,—
Powers of the impassioned hours prohibited.
Aye, clench the casket now! Whither they go
Thou mayst not dare to think: nor canst thou know
If Hope still pent there be alive or dead.

Penumbra

I did not look upon her eyes,
(Though scarcely seen, with no surprise,
'Mid many eyes a single look,)
Because they should not gaze rebuke,
At night, from stars in sky and brook.
I did not take her by the hand,
(Though little was to understand
From touch of hand all friends might take,)
Because it should not prove a flake
Burnt in my palm to boil and ache.
I did not listen to her voice,
(Though none had noted, where at choice
All might rejoice in listening,)
Because no such a thing should cling
In the wood's moan at evening.
I did not cross her shadow once,
(Though from the hollow west the sun's
Last shadow runs along so far,)
Because in June it should not bar
My ways, at noon when fevers are.
They told me she was sad that day,
(Though wherefore tell what love's soothsay,
Sooner than they, did register?)
And my heart leapt and wept to her,
And yet I did not speak nor stir.
So shall the tongues of the sea's foam
(Though many voices therewith come
From drowned hope's home to cry to me,)
Bewail one hour the more, when sea
And wind are one with memory.

Hidden Harmony

The thoughts in me are very calm and high
That think upon your love: yet by your leave
You shall not greatly marvel that this eve
Or nightfall—yet scarce nightfall—the strong sky
Leaves me thus sad. Now if you ask me why,
I cannot teach you, dear; but I believe
It is that man will always interweave
Life with fresh want, with wish or fear to die.
It may be therefore,—though the matter touch
Nowise our love,—that I so often look
Sad in your presence, often feeling so.
And of the reason I can tell thus much:—
Man's soul is like the music in a book
Which were not music but for high and low.

Insomnia

Thin are the night-skirts left behind
By daybreak hours that onward creep,
And thin, alas! the shred of sleep
That wavers with the spirit's wind:
But in half-dreams that shift and roll
And still remember and forget,
My soul this hour has drawn your soul
A little nearer yet.

Our lives, most dear, are never near,
Our thoughts are never far apart,
Though all that draws us heart to heart
Seems fainter now and now more clear.
To-night Love claims his full control,
And with desire and with regret
My soul this hour has drawn your soul
A little nearer yet.

Is there a home where heavy earth
Melts to bright air that breathes no pain,
Where water leaves no thirst again
And springing fire is Love's new birth?
If faith long bound to one true goal
May there at length its hope beget,
My soul that hour shall draw your soul
For ever nearer yet.

Aspecta Medusa (for a Drawing)

Andromeda, by Perseus sav'd and wed,
Hanker'd each day to see the Gorgon's head:
Till o'er a fount he held it, bade her lean,
And mirror'd in the wave was safely seen
That death she liv'd by.

Let not thine eyes know
Any forbidden thing itself, although
It once should save as well as kill: but be
Its shadow upon life enough for thee.

Jenny

"Vengeance of Jenny's case! Fie on her! Never name her, child!" —Mrs. Quickly

Lazy laughing languid Jenny,
Fond of a kiss and fond of a guinea,
Whose head upon my knee to-night
Rests for a while, as if grown light
With all our dances and the sound
To which the wild tunes spun you round:
Fair Jenny mine, the thoughtless queen
Of kisses which the blush between
Could hardly make much daintier;
Whose eyes are as blue skies, whose hair
Is countless gold incomparable:
Fresh flower, scarce touched with signs that tell
Of Love's exuberant hotbed:—Nay,
Poor flower left torn since yesterday
Until to-morrow leave you bare;
Poor handful of bright spring-water
Flung in the whirlpool's shrieking face;
Poor shameful Jenny, full of grace
Thus with your head upon my knee;—
Whose person or whose purse may be
The lodestar of your reverie?

This room of yours, my Jenny, looks
A change from mine so full of books,
Whose serried ranks hold fast, forsooth,
So many captive hours of youth,—
The hours they thieve from day and night
To make one's cherished work come right,

And leave it wrong for all their theft,
Even as to-night my work has left:
Until I vowed that since my brain
And eyes of dancing seemed so fain,
My feet should have some dancing too:—
And thus it was I met with you.
Well, I suppose 'twas hard to part,
For here I am. And now, sweetheart,
You seem too tired to get to bed.

It was a careless life I led
When rooms like this were scarce so strange
Not long ago. What breeds the change,—
The many aims or the few years?
Because to-night it all appears
Something I do not know again.

The   cloud's not danced out of my brain,—
The cloud that made it turn and swim
While hour by hour the books grew dim.
Why, Jenny, as I watch you there,—
For all your wealth of loosened hair,
Your silk ungirdled and unlac'd
And warm sweets open to the waist,
All golden in the lamplight's gleam,—
You know not what a book you seem,
Half-read by lightning in a dream!
How should you know, my Jenny? Nay,
And I should be ashamed to say:—
Poor beauty, so well worth a kiss!
But while my thought runs on like this
With wasteful whims more than enough,
I wonder what you're thinking of.

If of myself you think at all,
What is the thought?—conjectural
On sorry matters best unsolved?—
Or inly is each grace revolved
To fit me with a lure?—or (sad
To think!) perhaps you're merely glad
That I'm not drunk or ruffianly
And let you rest upon my knee.

For sometimes, were the truth confess'd,
You're thankful for a little rest,—
Glad from the crush to rest within,
From the heart-sickness and the din
Where envy's voice at virtue's pitch

Mocks you because your gown is rich;
And from the pale girl's dumb rebuke,
Whose ill-clad grace and toil-worn look
Proclaim the strength that keeps her weak,
And other nights than yours bespeak;
And from the wise unchildish elf,
To schoolmate lesser than himself
Pointing you out, what thing you are:—
Yes, from the daily jeer and jar,
From shame and shame's outbraving too,
Is rest not sometimes sweet to you?—
But most from the hatefulness of man
Who spares not to end what he began,
Whose acts are ill and his speech ill,
Who, having used you at his will,
Thrusts you aside, as when I dine
I serve the dishes and the wine.

Well, handsome Jenny mine, sit up:
I've filled our glasses, let us sup,
And do not let me think of you,
Lest shame of yours suffice for two.
What, still so tired? Well, well then, keep
Your head there, so you do not sleep;
But that the weariness may pass
And leave you merry, take this glass.
Ah! lazy lily hand, more bless'd
If ne'er in rings it had been dress'd
Nor ever by a glove conceal'd!

Behold the lilies of the field,
They toil not neither do they spin;
(So doth the ancient text begin,—
Not of such rest as one of these
Can share.) Another rest and ease.
Along each summer-sated path
From its new lord the garden hath,
Than that whose spring in blessings ran
Which praised the bounteous husbandman,
Ere yet, in days of hankering breath,
The lilies sickened unto death.

What, Jenny, are your lilies dead?
Aye, and the snow-white leaves are spread
Like winter on the garden-bed.
But you had roses left in May,—
They were not gone too. Jenny, nay,
But must your roses die, and those

Their purfled buds that should unclose?
Even so; the leaves are curled apart,
Still red as from the broken heart,
And here's the naked stem of thorns.

Nay, nay mere words. Here nothing warns
As yet of winter. Sickness here
Or want alone could waken fear,—
Nothing but passion wrings a tear.
Except when there may rise unsought
Haply at times a passing thought
Of the old days which seem to be
Much older than any history
That is written in any book;
When she would lie in fields and look
Along the ground through the blown grass,
And wonder where the city was,
Far out of sight, whose broil and bale
They told her then for a child's tale.

Jenny, you know the city now,
A child can tell the tale there, how
Some things which are not yet enroll'd
In market-lists are bought and sold
Even till the early Sunday light,
When Saturday night is market-night
Everywhere, be it dry or wet,
And market-night in the Haymarket.
Our learned London children know,
Poor Jenny, all your pride and woe;
Have seen your lifted silken skirt
Advertise dainties through the dirt;
Have seen your coach-wheels splash rebuke
On virtue; and have learned your look
When, wealth and health slipped past, you stare
Along the streets alone, and there,
Round the long park, across the bridge,
The cold lamps at the pavement's edge
Wind on together and apart,
A fiery serpent for your heart.

Let the thoughts pass, an empty cloud!
Suppose I were to think aloud,—
What if to her all this were said?
Why, as a volume seldom read
Being opened halfway shuts again,
So might the pages of her brain
Be parted at such words, and thence

Close back upon the dusty sense.
For is there hue or shape defin'd
In Jenny's desecrated mind,
Where all contagious currents meet,
A Lethe of the middle street?
Nay, it reflects not any face,
Nor sound is in its sluggish pace,
But as they coil those eddies clot,
And night and day remembers not.

Why, Jenny, you're asleep at last!—
Asleep, poor Jenny, hard and fast,—
So young and soft and tired; so fair,
With chin thus nestled in your hair,
Mouth quiet, eyelids almost blue
As if some sky of dreams shone through!

Just as another woman sleeps!
Enough to throw one's thoughts in heaps
Of doubt and horror,—what to say
Or think,—this awful secret sway,
The potter's power over the clay!
Of the same lump (it has been said)
For honour and dishonour made,
Two sister vessels. Here is one.

My cousin Nell is fond of fun,
And fond of dress, and change, and praise,
So mere a woman in her ways:
And if her sweet eyes rich in youth
Are like her lips that tell the truth,
My cousin Nell is fond of love.
And she's the girl I'm proudest of.
Who does not prize her, guard her well?
The love of change, in cousin Nell,
Shall find the best and hold it dear:
The unconquered mirth turn quieter
Not through her own, through others' woe:
The conscious pride of beauty glow
Beside another's pride in her,
One little part of all they share.
For Love himself shall ripen these
In a kind of soil to just increase
Through years of fertilizing peace.

Of the same lump (as it is said)
For honour and dishonour made,
Two sister vessels. Here is one.

It makes a goblin of the sun.

So pure,—so fall'n! How dare to think
Of the first common kindred link?
Yet, Jenny, till the world shall burn
It seems that all things take their turn;
And who shall say but this fair tree
May need, in changes that may be,
Your children's children's charity?
Scorned then, no doubt, as you are scorn'd!
Shall no man hold his pride forewarn'd
Till in the end, the Day of Days,
At Judgement, one of his own race,
As frail and lost as you, shall rise,—
His daughter, with his mother's eyes?

How Jenny's clock ticks on the shelf!
Might not the dial scorn itself
That has such hours to register?
Yet as to me, even so to her
Are golden sun and silver moon,
In daily largesse of earth's boon,
Counted for life-coins to one tune.
And if, as blindfold fates are toss'd,
Through some one man this life be lost,
Shall soul not somehow pray for soul?

Fair shines the gilded aureole
In which our highest painters place
Some living woman's simple face.
And the stilled features thus descried
As Jenny's long throat droops aside,—
The shadows where the cheeks are thin,
And pure wide curve from ear to chin,—
Whit Raffael's, Leonardo's hand
To show them to men's souls, might stand,
Whole ages long, the whole world through,
For preachings of what God can do.
What has man done here? How atone,
Great God, for this which man has done?
And for the body and soul which by
Man's pitiless doom must now comply
With lifelong hell, what lullaby
Of sweet forgetful second birth
Remains? All dark. No sign on earth
What measure of God's rest endows
The many mansions of his house.

If but a woman's heart might see
Such erring heart unerringly
For once! But that can never be.

Like a rose shut in a book
In which pure women may not look,
For its base pages claim control
To crush the flower within the soul;
Where through each dead rose-leaf that clings,
Pale as transparent psyche-wings,
To the vile text, are traced such things
As might make lady's cheek indeed
More than a living rose to read;
So nought save foolish foulness may
Watch with hard eyes the sure decay;
And so the life-blood of this rose,
Puddled with shameful knowledge, flows
Through leaves no chaste hand may unclose:
Yet still it keeps such faded show
Of when 'twas gathered long ago,
That the crushed petals' lovely grain,
The sweetness of the sanguine stain,
Seen of a woman's eyes, must make
Her pitiful heart, so prone to ache,
Love roses better for its sake:—
Only that this can never be:—
Even so unto her sex is she.

Yet, Jenny, looking long at you,
The woman almost fades from view.
A cipher of man's changeless sum
Of lust, past, present, and to come,
Is left. A riddle that one shrinks
To challenge from the scornful sphinx.

Like a toad within a stone
Seated while Time crumbles on;
Which sits there since the earth was curs'd
For Man's transgression at the first;
Which, living through all centuries,
Not once has seen the sun arise;
Whose life, to its cold circle charmed,
The earth's whole summers have not warmed;
Which always—whitherso the stone
Be flung—sits there, deaf, blind, alone;—
Aye, and shall not be driven out
Till that which shuts him round about

Break at the very Master's stroke,
And the dust thereof vanish as smoke,
And the seed of Man vanish as dust:—
Even so within this world is Lust.

Come, come, what use in thoughts like this?
Poor little Jenny, good to kiss,—
You'd not believe by what strange roads
Thought travels, when your beauty goads
A man to-night to think of toads!
Jenny, wake up. . . . Why, there's the dawn!

And there's an early waggon drawn
To market, and some sheep that jog
Bleating before a barking dog;
And the old streets come peering through
Another night that London knew;
And all as ghostlike as the lamps.

So on the wings of day decamps
My last night's frolic. Glooms begin
To shiver off as lights creep in
Past the gauze curtains half drawn-to,
And the lamp's doubled shade grows blue,—
Your lamp, my Jenny, kept alight,
Like a wise virgin's, all one night!
And in the alcove coolly spread
Glimmers with dawn your empty bed;
And yonder your fair face I see
Reflected lying on my knee,
Where teems with first foreshadowings
Your pier-glass scrawled with diamond rings:
And on your bosom all night worn
Yesterday's rose now droops forlorn,
But dies not yet this summer morn.

And now without, as if some word
Had called upon them that they heard,
The London sparrows far and nigh
Clamour together suddenly;
And Jenny's cage-bird grown awake
Here in their song his part must take,
Because here too the day doth break.

And somehow in myself the dawn
Among stirred clouds and veils withdrawn
Strikes greyly on her. Let her sleep.
But will it wake her if I heap

These cushions thus beneath her head
Where my knee was? No,—there's your bed,
My Jenny, while you dream. And there
I lay among your golden hair
Perhaps the subject of your dreams,
These golden coins.
For still one deems
That Jenny's flattering sleep confers
New magic on the magic purse,—
Grim web, how clogged with shrivelled flies!
Between the threads fine fumes arise
And shape their pictures in the brain.
There roll no streets in glare and rain,
Nor flagrant man-swine whets his tusk;
But delicately sighs in musk
The homage of the dim boudoir;
Or like a palpitating star
Thrilled into song, the opera-night
Breathes faint in the quick pulse of light;
Or at the carriage-window shine
Rich wares for choice; or, free to dine,
Whirls through its hour of health (divine
For her) the concourse of the Park.
And though in the discounted dark
Her functions there and here are one,
Beneath the lamps and in the sun
There reigns at least the acknowledged belle
Apparelled beyond parallel.
Ah Jenny, yes, we know your dreams.

For even the Paphian Venus seems,
A goddess o'er the realms of love,
When silver-shrined in shadowy grove:
Aye, or let offerings nicely placed
But hide Priapus to the waist,
And whoso looks on him shall see
An eligible deity.

Why, Jenny, waking here alone
May help you to remember one,
Though all the memory's long outworn
Of many a double-pillowed morn.
I think I see you when you wake,
And rub your eyes for me, and shake
My gold, in rising, from your hair,
A Danaë for a moment there.

Jenny, my love rang true! for still

Love at first sight is vague, until
That tinkling makes him audible.

And must I mock you to the last,
Ashamed of my own shame,—aghast
Because some thoughts not born amiss
Rose at a poor fair face like this?
Well, of such thoughts so much I know:
In my life, as in hers, they show,
By a far gleam which I may near,
A dark path I can strive to clear.

Only one kiss. Good-bye, my dear.